Holy Hour of Reparation To The Sacred Heart of Jesus

For Neglect Of and Negligence In Priestly and Religious Vocations

Booklet: Sensus Traditionis Press.
For additional copies: http://sensustraditionispress.org

Front cover: Sacred Heart of Jesus. Copyright © 2004
Marian Catechist Apostolate. (Prints and holy cards available
from Marian Catechist Bookstore, 608-782-0011
or www.MarianCatechist.com.)

Contents

Preface

"Behold this Heart which has so loved men that it has spared nothing, even to exhausting and consuming itself, in order to testify its love. In return, from the greater part I receive only ingratitude."

These are the words of Our Divine Master to St. Margaret Mary Alacoque. It gives pain to the heart to know that Our Divine Master has to complain. And what is His complaint? The lack of gratitude and the lack of love for His Sacred Heart.

In other places we also see the desire of the Sacred Heart for an increase both of quality and quantity in vocations to the priesthood and religious life.

The beauty of this Holy Hour is that, responding to the initial request of Our Redeemer in the Garden: *"Could you not watch one hour with me"*, it attempts to respond to that complaint of the Divine Heart and do reparation in these three areas. It seeks to do reparation for the neglect and tepidity of and in vocations, it expresses gratitude for the many benefits that we have been blessed with, and it expresses our devotion to the Sacred Heart.

The average person will pray many prayers of petition in times of need and only a few prayers of thanksgiving after a prayer has been answered. It does not occur to us to pray prayers of gratitude for the Divine Mysteries, the blessings and graces of Redemption and the mysteries of the Divine Attributes. Even the crosses that we blame God for giving us are a means of sanctification and merit that we seldom give Him thanks for. We should show gratitude for the manner in which He can extract good even out of these evils and bestow great blessings on us!

We take too much for granted, so much so that the Divine Heart has to gently complain: *"From the greater part I receive only ingratitude"*.

In this Holy Hour we put ourselves aside. We put our needs and concerns and wants on the back burner. We fill our prayer with something more important: the Divine Heart of our Savior. We give Him our attention, our love, our reparation, our adoration, and our gratitude.

And as we pray these prayers, we pray for an intention that is dear to Him: for vocations and for the sanctification of priests and religious. How few there are that respond to the Divine Call in our day and dedicate their lives to His service! How sad it is to see many of those who are consecrated to Him consider their lives as social work and are not filled with the love that comes from His Heart! How we should pray that their fervor is increased and that they serve Him as they set out to do when they left all to follow Him! That they remain faithful to obedience and to the truths of our faith and not neglect their duty, according to Pope St. Gregory the Great, to preach those truths with clarity! This Holy Hour serves the purpose of reparation for the sorrow caused to the Divine Heart by this lukewarmness and neglect in His chosen souls and prays for an increase in the fervor of their vocations.

We truly give this hour to the Good Lord. We do not nag Him for an hour about our own needs and wants; instead we fill an hour with His needs and His wants. The beauty of this Holy Hour is that it fulfills that golden rule of good Liturgy and genuine prayer: *it's not about us, it's about Him.*

One of the mysteries of the Divine Heart of Our Savior is that He loves us more than we could ever love Him. He knows our needs more than we could ever express them. As we pray this Holy Hour of Reparation, Our Lord will bless us with His help in our needs. He will provide for us, not only in the minor things that we are most concerned about, but also in the more important things such as our sanctification, the assistance in practicing virtue, a growth in the love of God, and all the needs of our family and loved ones. It is humbling to know that the more love we give the Good Lord, so much the more love He showers upon us, and the more gratitude we show Him the more He blesses us. As the Divine Child said to Fr Cyrillus: *"the more you honor Me, the more I will bless you!"*

Take an hour out of your week and give it to Our Divine Master by praying this Holy Hour of Reparation. Don't do it to get something out of it; it's time to give back something to Him. Show that Heart some love, who has shown you so much love. Give that Heart some gratitude, who has given so much to you.

Rev. Fr. J. Fryar FSSP

Introduction

The Holy Hour is divided into three parts:

1. The first 30 **minutes**: Prayer **of Intention and Prayers of Gratitude** to God
2. Next 30 minutes: **Prayers of Reparation to the Sacred Heart**
3. An additional 3-5 minutes: **Prayers of Petition**

The Holy Hour can be done during exposition of the Blessed Sacrament, in front of the tabernacle, or at home for the home bound. (The preferred time is between the hours of 9 p.m. and 5 a.m., if possible, because this is when Our Lord is most offended.)

Part 1: Prayer of Intention and Prayers of Gratitude

Prayer for the Intention of this Holy Hour

O Mary, who accompanied thy Son during His sacrifice upon the Cross, I humbly ask thee to present thy tears and thy sorrows that thou underwent during the Passion to thy Son's Sacred Heart in reparation for the neglect of and negligence in priestly and religious vocations. In turn, Queen of Confessors, I offer thee this hour of reparation so that thou may purify it and present it to thy Son in reparation for these offenses and for our failure to pray and do penance for priests and religious so that they may fulfill their vocations and accomplish the duties of their state. I offer this hour to make amendment to thy Immaculate Heart, which, with burning charity, loves those who have accepted their vocations but who daily suffer insults from the world and even from within the Church. Queen of the Clergy, we beg thee to petition thy Son for all of the graces necessary for those who are discerning their vocations lest they neglect them. Amen.

Prayers of Gratitude

Our Beloved Mother, I thank thee for the graces that thou hast given to the priests and religious throughout the world whose daily sacrifices are the means of our sanctification. Amen.

Oh my soul, bless the Lord, and everything within me, bless His Holy Name, and forget not, my soul, the favors He has bestowed upon thee.

Prayers of gratitude are prayers of thanksgiving to God for all that He is, all that He has created, and all that He has done, not only for us, but for all.

A sample format that may be followed for additional prayers of gratitude:

Thank Our Lord for one or more specific attributes of God, Our Lady, etc., such as those listed below, or for gifts we have received, followed by a short prayer. (Examples are given on the facing page.) This format is repeated over the 30 minute period.

Short List of Gifts For Which to Show Gratitude

These are broad general categories; much can be expanded and detailed.

- Attributes and excellence of God
- Three Divine Persons in His Trinity, Father, Son, and Holy Ghost
- Jesus in His Nativity
- His Passion, Death, and Resurrection
- His Ascension
- Our Redemption
- His Justice and Mercy
- All of His attributes in each Person and as One.
- His creation
- The world
- The heavens
- The angels
- Our Blessed Mother
- Her Immaculate Conception
- Her perpetual virginity
- Her life, death and Assumption
- All She did in this world
- All She does as Queen of Heaven
- All She does as our heavenly mother
- All Her attributes, such as Her perfections
- Her Immaculate Heart
- Her purity
- Her humility
- Her charity
- The Saints
- Their virtues and examples
- All He has done through them
- For ourselves
- His Church
- The Sacraments
- The Sacraments we have received, especially Baptism
- All He has done through us, especially leading others to God
- All of our temporal gifts
- Our guardian angels
- Our family, friends, priests, etc.
- All God has given them
- All God does through them
- All of our spiritual gifts, and favors granted
- Prayer, especially mental prayer and contemplation
- Detachment from things of the world
- Adversity and all of our crosses

Short Prayers of Gratitude

Below are several short prayers which may be offered, although any other heartfelt prayers will also please Our Lord:

- Glory be to the Father and to the Son and to the Holy Spirit, as it was in the beginning, is now, and ever shall be world without end. Amen. (Gloria Patri)

- Blessed be the Name of the Lord!

- Abide with me, O Lord; be Thou my true joy.

- Blessing and glory and wisdom and thanksgiving, honor, might and power be unto our God forever and ever.

- Eternal God, Thou showeth us Thy perfections through Thy creation.

- All through Thee, with Thee, and in Thee, O my God!

- Lord I am nothing, but although nothing, I adore Thee.

- Blessed be Jesus and His most pure Mother!

- Jesus, grant that I may be Thine, wholly Thine, forever Thine.

- I adore Thee every moment, O living Bread from Heaven, Great Sacrament.

- Hail O Cross, our only hope!

- Jesus, meek and humble of heart, make our hearts like unto Thine.

- Glory, love and thanksgiving be to the Sacred Heart of Jesus.

- Sacred Heart of Jesus, I give myself to Thee through Mary.

- Before the angels I will sing praise unto Thee, O my God!

- My God I love Thee.

- God grant him/her peace and joy in this world and eternal happiness in the next!

- Eternal Father, I give Thee my most humble thanks and gratitude for these.

"Oh, Divine Heart.....

...I wish to love Thee with my
whole heart."

Part 2: Prayers of Reparation

Please pray the Act of Reparation to the Sacred Heart and Prayer to the Sacred Heart for Priests (below).

Any additional prayers to the Sacred Heart may follow. Examples are provided. Other prayers can be found in *The Devotion to the Sacred Heart of Jesus: How to Practice the Sacred Heart Devotion*, Rev. Fr. John Croiset, and other devotional books and Catholic prayer books.

Act of Reparation (Actus Reparationis)

A partial indulgence is granted to those who recite this prayer. A plenary indulgence is granted if it is publicly recited on the feast of the Most Sacred Heart of Jesus. This prayer was prescribed to be recited on this feast by Pope Pius XI.

IESU dulcissime, cuius effusa in homines caritas, tanta oblivione, negligentia, contemptione, ingratissime rependitur, en nos, ante altaria tua provoluti, tam nefariam hominum socordiam iniuriasque, quibus undique amantissimum Cor tuum afficitur, peculiari honore resarcire contendimus.

Attamen, memores tantae nos quoque indignitatis non expertes aliquando fuisse, indeque vehementissimo dolore commoti, tuam in primis misericordiam nobis imploramus, paratis, voluntaria expiatione compensare flagitia non modo quae ipsi patravimus, sed etiam illorum, qui, longe a salutis via aberrantes, vel te pastorem ducemque sectari detrectant, in sua infidelitate obstinati, vel baptismatis

MOST sweet Jesus, whose overflowing charity for men is requited by so much forgetfulness, negligence and contempt, behold us prostrate before Thee, eager to repair by a special act of homage the cruel indifference and injuries to which Thy loving Heart is everywhere subject.

Mindful, alas! that we ourselves have had a share in such great indignities, which we now deplore from the depths of our hearts, we humbly ask Thy pardon and declare our readiness to atone by voluntary expiation, not only for our own personal offenses, but also for the sins of those, who, straying far from the path of salvation, refuse in their obstinate infidelity to follow Thee, their Shepherd and Leader, or,

promissa conculcantes, suavissimum tuae legis iugum excusserunt.

Quae deploranda crimina, cum universa expiare contendimus, tum nobis singula resarcienda proponimus: vitae cultusque immodestiam atque turpitudines, tot corruptelae pedicas innocentium animis instructas, dies festos violatos, exsecranda in te tuosque Sanctos iactata maledicta atque in tuum Vicarium ordinemque sacerdotalem convicia irrogata, ipsum denique amoris divini Sacramentum, vel neglectum vel horrendis sacrilegiis profanatum, publica postremo nationum delicta, quae Ecclesiae a te institutae iuribus magisterioque reluctantur.

Quae utinam crimina sanguine ipsi nostro eluere possemus! Interea ad violatum divinum honorem resarciendum, quam Tu olim Patri in Cruce satisfactionem obtulisti quamque quotidie in Altaribus renova repergis, hanc eandem nos tibi praestamus, cum Virginis Matris, omnium Sanctorum, piorum quoque fidelium expiationibus coniunctam, ex animo spondentes, cum praeterita nostra aliorumque peccata ac tanti

renouncing the promises of their baptism, have cast off the sweet yoke of Thy law.

We are now resolved to expiate each and every deplorable outrage committed against Thee; we are now determined to make amends for the manifold offenses against Christian modesty in unbecoming dress and behavior, for all the foul seductions laid to ensnare the feet of the innocent, for the frequent violations of Sundays and holydays, and the shocking blasphemies uttered against Thee and Thy Saints. We wish also to make amends for the insults to which Thy Vicar on earth and Thy priests are subjected, for the profanation, by conscious neglect or terrible acts of sacrilege of the very Sacrament of Thy Divine Love, and lastly for the public crimes of nations who resist the rights and teaching authority of the Church which Thou hast founded.

Would that we were able to wash away such abominations with our blood. We now offer, in reparation for these violations of Thy divine honor, the satisfaction Thou once made to Thy Eternal Father on the Cross and which Thou continuest to renew daily on our Altars; we offer it in union with the acts of atonement of Thy Virgin Mother and all the Saints and of the pious faithful on earth; and we sincerely

amoris incuriam firma fide, candidis vitae moribus, perfecta legis evangelicae, caritatis potissimum, observantia, quantum in nobis erit, gratia tua favente, nos esse compensaturos, tum iniurias tibi inferendas pro viribus prohibituros, et quam plurimos potuerimus ad tui sequelam convocaturos.

promise to make recompense, as far as we can with the help of Thy grace, for all neglect of Thy great love and for the sins we and others have committed in the past. Henceforth, we will live a life of unswerving faith, of purity of conduct, of perfect observance of the precepts of the Gospel and especially that of charity. We promise to the best of our power to prevent others from offending Thee and to bring as many as possible to follow Thee.

Excipias, quaesumus, benignissime Iesu, beata Virgine Maria Reparatrice intercedente, voluntarium huius expiationis obsequium nosque in officio tuique servito fidissimos ad mortem usque velis, magno illo perseverantiae munere, continere, ut ad illam tandem patriam perveniamus omnes ubi Tu cum Patre et Spiritu Sancto vivis et regnas in saecula saeculorum. Amen.

O loving Jesus, through the intercession of the Blessed Virgin Mother, our model in reparation, deign to receive the voluntary offering we make of this act of expiation; and by the crowning gift of perseverance keep us faithful unto death in our duty and the allegiance we owe to Thee, so that we may all one day come to that happy home, where with the Father and the Holy Spirit Thou livest and reignest, God, forever and ever. Amen.

Prayer to the Sacred Heart for Priests

Remember, O most loving Heart of Jesus, that they for whom I pray are those for whom You prayed so earnestly the night before Your death. These are they to whom You look to continue with You in Your sorrows when others forsake You, who share Your griefs and have inherited Your persecutions, according to Your word: That the servant is not greater than his Lord. Remember, O Heart of Jesus, that they are the objects of the world's hatred and Satan's deadliest snares.

Keep them then, O Jesus, in the safe citadel of Your Sacred Heart and there let them be sanctified in truth. May they be one with You and one among themselves, and grant that multitudes may be brought through their word to believe in You and love You.

Renewal of the Consecration of the Family

Most sweet Jesus, humbly kneeling at Thy feet, we renew the consecration of our family to Thy Divine Heart. Be Thou our King forever! In Thee we have full and entire confidence. May Thy spirit penetrate our thoughts, our desires, our words and our works. Bless our undertakings, share in our joys, in our trials and in our labors. Grant us to know Thee better, to love Thee more, and to serve Thee without faltering.

By the Immaculate Heart of Mary, Queen of Peace, set up Thy kingdom in our country. Enter closely into the midst of our families and make them Thine own through the solemn enthronement of Thy Sacred Heart, so that soon one cry may resound from home to home: "May the triumphant Heart of Jesus be everywhere loved, blessed and glorified forever!" Honor and glory to the Sacred Hearts of Jesus and Mary!

Act of Love to the Sacred Heart

O most loving Heart of my only love Jesus, not being able to love, honor, and glorify Thee according to the extent of the desire which Thou hast given me to do so, I invite Heaven and earth to join with me; I unite myself with the burning Seraphim to love Thee. O Heart all burning with love, mayest Thou inflame Heaven and earth with Thy most pure flames and consume all that they contain, in order that all creatures may breathe only by Thy love! Grant me either to die or to suffer, or at least change me completely and make me all heart in order to love Thee, consuming myself in Thy burning ardor. O divine fire, O all pure flames of the Heart of my only love Jesus, burn me without pity, consume me and I will not resist. Oh! why dost Thou spare me since I deserve only fire and since I am fit only for burning? O Love of Heaven and earth, come, come into my heart and inflame me! O devouring fire of Divinity, come, descend upon me! Burn me, consume me in the midst of Thy most lively flames which make those live who die in them. Amen.

Litany of the Sacred Heart of Jesus *(Litaniae de Sacratissimo Corde Iesu)*

In 1899 Pope Leo XIII approved this Litany of the Sacred Heart of Jesus for public use. This litany is actually a synthesis of several other litanies dating back to the 17th century. Father Croiset composed a litany in 1691 from which 17 invocations were used by Venerable Anne Madeleine Remuzat when she composed her litany in 1718 at Marseilles. She joined an additional 10 invocations to those of Father Croiset, for a total of 27 invocations. Six more invocations written by Sister Madeleine Joly of Dijon in 1686 were added by the Sacred Congregation for Rites when it was approved for public use in 1899. This makes a total of 33 invocations, one for each year of life of our Lord Jesus Christ. A partial indulgence is attached to this litany.

Kyrie, eleison
R. Kyrie, eleison.

Lord, have mercy
R. Lord, have mercy.

Christe, eleison
R. Christe, eleison.

Christ, have mercy
R. Christ, have mercy.

Kyrie, eleison
R. Kyrie, eleison.

Lord, have mercy
R. Lord, have mercy.

Christe, audi nos
R. Christe, audi nos.

Christ, hear us
R. Christ, hear us.

Christe, exaudi nos.
R. Christe, exaudi nos.

Christ, graciously hear us.
R. Christ, graciously hear us.

Pater de caelis, Deus,*

God the Father of Heaven,*

Fili, Redemptor mundi, Deus,

God the Son, Redeemer of the world,

Spiritus Sancte, Deus,

God, the Holy Spirit,

Sancta Trinitas, unus Deus,

Holy Trinity, One God,

Cor Iesu, Filii Patris aeterni,

Heart of Jesus, Son of the Eternal Father,

*miserere nobis

*have mercy on us

Cor Iesu, in sinu Virginis Matris a Spiritu Sancto formatum,*	Heart of Jesus, formed by the Holy Spirit in the womb of the Virgin Mother,*
Cor Iesu, Verbo Dei substantialiter unitum,	Heart of Jesus, substantially united to the Word of God,
Cor Iesu, maiestatis infinitae,	Heart of Jesus, of Infinite Majesty,
Cor Iesu, templum Dei sanctum,	Heart of Jesus, Sacred Temple of God,
Cor Iesu, tabernaculum Altissimi,	Heart of Jesus, Tabernacle of the Most High,
Cor Iesu, domus Dei et porta caeli,	Heart of Jesus, House of God and Gate of Heaven,
Cor Iesu, fornax ardens caritatis,	Heart of Jesus, burning furnace of charity,
Cor Iesu, iustitiae et amoris receptaculum,	Heart of Jesus, abode of justice and love,
Cor Iesu, bonitate et amore plenum,	Heart of Jesus, full of goodness and love,
Cor Iesu, virtutum omnium abyssus,	Heart of Jesus, abyss of all virtues,
Cor Iesu, omni laude dignissimum	Heart of Jesus, most worthy of all praise,
Cor Iesu, rex et centrum omnium cordium,	Heart of Jesus, king and center of all hearts,
Cor Iesu, in quo sunt omnes thesauri sapientiae et scientiae,	Heart of Jesus, in whom are all treasures of wisdom and knowledge,
Cor Iesu, in quo habitat omnis plenitudo divinitatis,	Heart of Jesus, in whom dwelleth the fullness of divinity,

*miserere nobis   ***have mercy on us**

Cor Iesu, in quo Pater sibi bene complacuit,*	Heart of Jesus, in whom the Father was well pleased,*
Cor Iesu, de cuius plenitudine omnes nos accepimus,	Heart of Jesus, of whose fullness we have all received,
Cor Iesu, desiderium collium aeternorum,	Heart of Jesus, desire of the everlasting hills,
Cor Iesu, patiens et multae misericordiae,	Heart of Jesus, patient and most merciful,
Cor Iesu, dives in omnes qui invocant te,	Heart of Jesus, enriching all who invoke Thee,
Cor Iesu, fons vitae et sanctitatis,	Heart of Jesus, fountain of life and holiness,
Cor Iesu, propitiatio pro peccatis nostris,	Heart of Jesus, propitiation for our sins,
Cor Iesu, saturatum opprobriis,	Heart of Jesus, loaded down with opprobrium,
Cor Iesu, attritum propter scelera nostra,	Heart of Jesus, bruised for our offenses,
Cor Iesu, usque ad mortem oboediens factum,	Heart of Jesus, obedient to death,
Cor Iesu, lancea perforatum,	Heart of Jesus, pierced with a lance,
Cor Iesu, fons totius consolationis,	Heart of Jesus, source of all consolation,
Cor Iesu, vita et resurrectio nostra,	Heart of Jesus, our life and resurrection,
Cor Iesu, pax et reconciliatio nostra,	Heart of Jesus, our peace and reconciliation,

*miserere nobis   ***have mercy on us**

Cor Iesu, victima peccatorum,*	Heart of Jesus, victim for our sins,*
Cor Iesu, salus in te sperantium,	Heart of Jesus, salvation of those who trust in Thee,
Cor Iesu, spes in te morientium,	Heart of Jesus, hope of those who die in Thee,
Cor Iesu, deliciae Sanctorum omnium,	Heart of Jesus, delight of all the Saints,
Agnus Dei, qui tollis peccata mundi,	Lamb of God, who takest away the sins of the world,
R. parce nobis, Domine.	R. spare us, O Lord.
Agnus Dei, qui tollis peccata mundi,	Lamb of God, who takest away the sins of the world,
R. exaudi nos, Domine.	R. graciously hear us, O Lord.
Agnus Dei, qui tollis peccata mundi,	Lamb of God, who takest away the sins of the world,
R. miserere nobis, Domine.	R. have mercy on us, O Lord.
V. Iesu, mitis et humilis Corde,	V. Jesus, meek and humble of heart.
R. Fac cor nostrum secundum Cor tuum.	R. Make our hearts like to Thine.

Oremus:
Omnipotens sempiterne Deus, respice in Cor dilectissimi Filii tui et in laudes et satisfactiones, quas in nomine peccatorum tibi persolvit, iisque misericordiam tuam petentibus, tu veniam concede placatus in nomine eiusdem Filii tui Iesu Christi: Qui tecum vivit et regnat in saecula saeculorum. **R.** Amen.

Let us pray:
Almighty and everlasting God, look upon the Heart of Thy well-beloved Son and upon the acts of praise and satisfaction which He renders unto Thee in the name of sinners; and do Thou, in Thy great goodness, grant pardon to them who seek Thy mercy, in the name of the same Thy Son, Jesus Christ, who liveth and reigneth with Thee, world without end. **R.** Amen.

*miserere nobis	***have mercy on us**

Beads of the Sacred Heart

As there is nothing so ingenious as love, several great saints in their great eagerness to make each day numerous acts of their favorite virtues according to the various inspirations of grace, have invented several kinds of chaplets composed of acts of these virtues.

After their example, the Beads of the Sacred Heart has been formed. It is composed of a crucifix, five large beads and thirty-three small ones in honor of the thirty-three years Our Lord spent on earth.

Instead of the Creed the following prayer may be said.

Soul of Jesus Christ, sanctify me.
Heart of Jesus, inflame me with love.
Body of Jesus Christ, save me.
Blood of Jesus Christ, inebriate me.
Water out of the Side of Christ, wash me.
Passion of Christ, strengthen me.
O good Jesus, hear me.
Within Thy Wounds, hide me.
Let me not be separated from Thee.
Defend me from the malignant enemy.
At the hour of death, call me.
And bid me to come unto Thee above,
That with the Saints, I may praise Thee for all eternity. Amen.

Before each large bead say:

Jesus most meek, make my heart like unto Thine.

On each large bead say:

We adore Thee, O Jesus, who hast been afflicted in the Garden of Gethsemani and who still in our time art outraged in the Blessed Sacrament by the impious conduct of men. O most amiable Saviour, we recognize that Thou alone art Holy, Thou alone art Lord, Thou alone art Most High.

On each small bead say:

I adore Thee, O most Sacred Heart of Jesus, inflame my heart with the divine love with which Thine Own is all on fire.

At the end of the beads say:
Our Father and a Hail Mary, and the following prayer:

O Lord Jesus Christ, who by an ineffable miracle of love, hast deigned to give Thy Heart to men to serve as their nourishment, in order thereby to gain their hearts, graciously hear our humble prayers, and pardon us for the sins of which we confess ourselves guilty before Thee. Cast an eye of compassion and mercy upon those towards whom Thou dost condescend to direct the affections of Thine amiable Heart. And since we desire to honor Thee in the adorable Mystery of the Altar to the utmost of our power and to render Thee most pleasing homage and for that intention, weep for and detest from the bottom of our hearts all the outrages, contempt, mockery, sacrileges, and other acts of impiety which ungrateful men in every part of the world have committed against Thee, enkindle therefore in our hearts this divine love with which Thine Own is inflamed, and inspire us with sentiments like unto Thine, in order that we may be able worthily to praise for all eternity the love with which this Sacred Heart burns for us. This is our prayer to Thee who livest and reignest with the Father, in unity of the Holy Spirit forever and ever. Amen

Prayers by St. Margaret Mary Alacoque

Act of Hope and Contrition

O Savior of my soul, I am under infinite obligations to Thy mercy, but I value nothing so highly as the desire for my salvation that consumes Thee. I confess that I owe Thee so much gratitude for so signal a favor and that I am under such an obligation to die to myself and to live and breathe only for Thee, that if I be wanting in this duty, I am unworthy of life. I, then, O Divine Redeemer, abandon myself entirely to Thee in life as in death. Make me live or die; I accept both with equal indifference provided that Thou dost not permit that either the one or the other ever separate me from Thee. O my only Hope, do not suffer that I be lost before Thine eyes after Thou hast saved me with so much pain. Alas! I do not know what is to become of me; but I know well that, as I can save myself by Thy grace, so I can damn myself by my own malice. I indeed hope for Thy grace, but my malice makes me fear and tremble. In this uncertainty, I have no other recourse but in the merits of Thy Cross; I embrace it with all my heart as the last plank after shipwreck. Oh! my Savior, honor Thy death by my salvation; render it glorious by my happiness; consume in me everything that is displeasing to Thee and fill up in me what is wanting to Thy sufferings; supply for me by Thy merits; make me such as Thou dost desire, in order that I may be able to recognize for all eternity the value of a God who dies for me, and what I owe to Thy death. Woe to that man who sees a God dying for his love and who does not cease to offend Him! I believe that Hell is too light a punishment for such ingratitude. How could I ever sin again when I think that God died on the Cross for me, after He had endured all torments, in order to teach me never to offend Him. Oh! my God, pardon this miserable sinner and force her to sin no more, but always and in all things to do Thy holy Will.

O my adorable Master, I detest my sins with the Heart of my Savior; I love my God with the Heart of His Son; as the Heart of Jesus has deplored my offenses, I deplore them. The tears which He shed with His eyes are mine, for Thou, O Eternal Father, hast given Him entirely to me, and I offer Thee His sorrow to supply for mine. If I have done evil, my Jesus has done good. Both are mine. If Thou dost regard the one, have regard to the other. I offer Thee His merits; in offering them to Thee, I give Thee more than I have taken away from Thee: for as the merits of my adorable Jesus infinitely exceed the malice of my sins, the good which He has done is greater than the evil which I have committed. Have pity then on me, O my God, and save me! I have placed all my hope in the Heart of Thy Divine Son; I will not be confounded. Amen.

Act of Contrition to the Sacred Heart of Jesus

O most Sacred and adorable Heart of Jesus, behold me humbly prostrate before Thee with a heart contrite and penetrated with lively sorrow for having loved Thee so little and for having offered Thee so many insults by my wandering from Thee, by my ingratitude, my perfidy and my other acts of infidelity, by which I have rendered myself unworthy of Thy mercies and of all the graces and favors of Thy pure love.

The shame and regret which I feel leave me no other words to express myself except to say: I have sinned against Thee. Have pity on me who am unworthy of all mercy. Do not condemn me, however, O Divine Heart, full of charity. I implore Thee to manifest the excess of Thy goodness by showing favor to this poor criminal who appears before Thee annihilated in the abyss of her nothingness and misery. Alas! O Sacred Heart, I have sinned against Thee; do not abandon me to the rigor of Thy justice which would infallibly punish any want of love towards Thee by the eternal privation of Thy love. Oh! rather let all torments, pains and miseries come and overwhelm me, than that I should be deprived for a moment of loving Thee! And since it is Thou, O Divine Heart of Jesus, the Source of love, who hast received the insults of all my infidelities and of my want of love, do Thou take care to be avenged upon me. If Thou wishest to condemn me to burn eternally, I consent, provided it be in the devouring fire of Thy pure love. O compassionate Heart, save me by the excess of Thy mercy. Do not allow me to perish in the deluge of my iniquities. O Heart of love, I cry to Thee from the abyss of my misery; save me by Thy ardent charity. Save me, I implore Thee, by all that is in Thee most capable of moving Thee to do me this great mercy. Have pity, then, on this poor criminal who expects her salvation from Thee.

Oh! save me, O merciful Heart, at whatever price it may cost. Save me and do not deprive me of loving Thee eternally. Rather let all the moments of life that remain to me be filled with bitterness, sorrow and affliction.

Am I not sufficiently punished for having loved so late a Heart so full of love! But because I love Thee, I have such regret for having so ungratefully offended Thee, my Sovereign Good, that rather than having committed so many sins, I would wish from the moment I commenced to sin to have endured as a preservative all the pains of Hell, although I hope that in Thy love Thou wilt exempt me from them. This is what I pray Thee, while crying to Thee with all my heart for mercy. Pardon, then, in Thy mercy, this afflicted heart which has put all its confidence and all its hope in Thee.

O Heart of Jesus, my Savior, exercise over me this office which has cost Thee so dear, and do not lose the fruit of so many sufferings and of so painful a death, but honor it by saving me in order that my heart may adore, praise and glorify Thee eternally. Be then, O Sacred Heart, our refuge and our hope, now and at the hour of our death!

Take my cause in hand, justify me and turn away the rigors which my sins have merited. Thou art my true friend; do Thou answer and satisfy for me. Draw me from the abyss into which my sins have precipitated me. Hearken to the groans of my afflicted heart which hopes for everything from Thy goodness. But if Thy justice condemns it as unworthy of pardon, it will appeal to the tribunal of Thy love, being ready to suffer all its rigors rather than be for a single moment deprived of loving Thee. Cut, burn, amputate; provided only I love Thee, it is sufficient for me. Spare neither my body nor my life, whenever there is question of Thy glory. I belong to Thee, O Divine and Adorable Heart, work out, then, my salvation, I implore Thee. In punishing my sins, do not abandon me to myself, allowing me to relapse into the same sins. Ah! rather a thousand deaths than offend Thee whom I love a hundred times more than my life!

What glory will the loss of a wretched grain of dust give Thee? And Thou shalt have great glory in saving such a miserable sinner. Save me, then, O pure Love, for I wish to love Thee eternally whatever price it may cost me. Yes, I wish to love Thee whatever it may cost me; I wish to love Thee with my whole heart. Amen.

Act of Love and Perfect Contrition

Humbly prostrate before Thee, O Sacred Heart of Jesus, I adore Thee, I praise Thee, I bless Thee, and I love Thee with all my strength and all the love of which my heart is capable; but do Thou extend its capacity and increase my love, in order that I may love Thee more, and that this love may make me belong completely to Thee forever. This is a grace which I ask for myself and for all hearts capable of loving, and especially for my own rebellious, hardened, unfaithful heart, which has so long abused Thy graces, resisted Thee and continued to offend Thee. I lead a life so cowardly in Thy service that, were it not for the excess of Thy mercy, Thou wouldst have long ago vomited me out of Thy mouth and rejected me as an object of horror and abomination which merits only to suffer eternally all the rigors of Thy just anger. But I implore Thee, O Sacred Heart of my adorable Jesus, by that ardent love and suffering on the tree of the Cross, and which will keep Thee in this state on our altars until the end of time, to grant me, poor, miserable sinner, pardon for all the sins that I have committed: my ingratitude, forgetfulness and infidelity, and the other insults that I have offered to Thee of which I repent with my whole heart. I ask Thy pardon with all the sorrow and regret of which I am capable, and I protest that I wish I could shed all my blood by all the torments imaginable, in order to satisfy Divine Justice and to repair the outrages which I have done to Thee. I accept in advance all the pains by which it may please Thee to chastise me in this life, and I beseech Thee not abandon me to myself and to sin and thus deprive me of Thy love. O Divine and most amiable Heart, do not condemn me to so horrible a torment as not to let all the pains of Hell come and torment me than that I should be for a single moment without loving Thee! O Divine Heart, Source of love and goodness, how couldst Thou forget Thy mercies and condemn to eternal privation of Thy love a heart which wishes henceforth in time and in eternity to live only to love Thee and to inhale and exhale breath only by this love.

Listen then, O most amiable Heart of my Lord Jesus Christ, to the prayer which I make and to the request which I present in my favor, wretched and unworthy sinner that I am; it is, that Thou wouldst grant me true conversion of heart. I detest all my past sins and I hold them in such horror that I would choose rather to be sunk in the abyss of Hell than relapse again in the future; and if Thou wishest to condemn me to flames, let it be to those of Thy pure love. Cast me into the abyss of this ardent furnace in punishment for all my perfidy. And when the excess of Thy goodness urges Thee to confer still further graces on me, I ask for no other than that of the sweet punishment of love. But grant, I implore Thee, that I may be consumed in this love and transformed into Thee. And in order to avenge Thyself on me for not loving Thee and for loving myself inordinately, pierce and transfix a thousand times my ungrateful heart with the dart of Thy pure love, that it may no longer be able to contain earthly and human love, but only the plenitude of Thy pure love, which will leave me no other liberty but that of loving Thee, while suffering and accomplishing in everything Thy holy will. These are the graces that I ask of Thee, O Sacred and most amiable Heart, and I implore Thee to grant them to me and to all hearts capable of loving Thee, and for them I ask Thee that they may live and die in this same love. Amen.

Little Act of Consecration to the Sacred Heart Of Jesus

I, _____, give and consecrate to the Sacred Heart of our Lord Jesus Christ, my person and my life, my actions, penances and sufferings, not wishing to make use of any part of my being for the future except in honoring, loving and glorifying that Sacred Heart.

It is my irrevocable will to be entirely His and to do everything for His love, and I renounce with my whole heart whatever might displease Him.

I take Thee, then, O most Sacred Heart, as the sole object of my love, as the protector of my life, as the pledge of my salvation, as the remedy of my frailty and inconstancy, as the repairer of all the defects of my life, and as my secure refuge at the hour of my death.

Be then, O Heart of Goodness, my justification before God the Father, and remove far from me the thunderbolts of His just wrath. O Heart of love I place my whole confidence in Thee. While I fear all things from my malice and frailty, I hope all things from Thy goodness.

Consume then in me whatever can displease or be opposed to Thee, and may Thy pure love be so deeply impressed on my heart that it may be impossible that I should ever be separated from Thee or forget Thee.

I implore Thee, by Thy goodness, that my name may be written in Thee, for in Thee I wish to place all my happiness and all my glory, living and dying in very bondage to Thee. Amen.

Invocations to the Heart of Jesus

Heart of Jesus in the Eucharist, Sweet Companion of our exile, I adore Thee.
Eucharistic Heart of Jesus, I adore Thee.
Heart solitary, Heart humiliated, I adore Thee.
Heart abandoned, Heart forgotten, I adore Thee.
Heart despised, Heart outraged, I adore Thee.
Heart ignored by men, I adore Thee.
Heart, Lover of our hearts, I adore Thee.
Heart pleading for love, I adore Thee.
Heart patient in waiting for us, I adore Thee.
Heart eager to hear our prayers, I adore Thee.
Heart desiring that we should pray to Thee, I adore Thee.
Heart, Source of fresh graces, I adore Thee.
Heart silent, desiring to speak to souls, I adore Thee.
Heart, Sweet Refuge of the hidden life, I adore Thee.
Heart, Teacher of the secrets of union with God, I adore Thee.
Heart of Him Who sleeps, yet ever watches, I adore Thee.
Eucharistic Heart of Jesus, have mercy on us.
Jesus Victim, I wish to comfort Thee; I unite myself to Thee;
I offer myself in union with Thee.
I count myself as nothing before Thee;
I desire to forget myself in order to think of Thee, to be forgotten and despised
        for love of Thee, not to be understood, not to be loved, except by Thee.
I will hold my peace that I may listen to Thee; I will forsake myself that I may
        lose myself in Thee.

Grant that I may quench Thy thirst for my salvation, Thy burning thirst for my sanctification, and that, being purified, I may bestow on Thee a pure and true love. I would no longer weary Thine expectations; take me, I give myself to Thee. I entrust to Thee all my actions---my mind that Thou mayest enlighten it, my heart that Thou mayest direct it, my will that Thou mayest establish it, my misery that Thou mayest relieve it, my soul and my body that Thou mayest feed them.

Eucharistic Heart of my Jesus, Whose Blood is the life of my soul, may it be no longer I who live, but Thou alone Who livest in me. Amen.

More Invocations

Hail, Sacred Heart of Jesus, living and strengthening source of eternal life, infinite treasury of the Divinity, and burning furnace of divine love! Unite my will with Yours that our wills may be one, and my will may in all things be conformed to Your Will. May Your Will be the guide and rule of my desires and of my actions. Amen.

Most holy Heart of Jesus, fountain of every blessing, I love You. With a lively sorrow for my sins I offer You this poor heart of mine. Make me humble, patient, and pure, and perfectly obedient to Your Will. Amen.

Good Jesus, grant that I may live in You and for You. Protect me in the midst of danger and comfort me in my afflictions. Bestow on me health of body, assistance in temporal needs, Your blessing on all that I do, and the grace of a holy death. Amen.

O Lord Jesus Christ, whose whole life was one continual sacrifice for the glory of Your Father and the salvation of our souls, grant us the grace to find our joy in making sacrifices for You and for the interests of Your Sacred Heart. Amen.

O Sacred Heart of Jesus, filled with infinite Love, broken by our ingratitude and pierced by our sins; yet loving us still; accept the consecration we make to Thee of all that we are and all that we have. Amen.

Take every faculty of our souls and bodies, only day by day draw us nearer and nearer to Thy Sacred Heart; and there as we shall hear the lesson, teach us Thy Holy Way. Amen.

Hail, Sacred Heart of Jesus, living and strengthening source of eternal life, infinite treasury of the Divinity, and burning furnace of divine love! You are my refuge and my sanctuary. Amen.

My loving Savior, consume my heart in that burning love with which Your own Heart is inflamed. Pour out upon me those graces which flow from Your Love. Let my heart be so united with Yours that our wills may be one, and my will may in all things be conformed to Your Will. May Your Will be the guide and rule of my desires and of my actions. Amen.

A Traditional Prayer of Reparation

Most loving Jesus, when I consider Your tender Heart and see It full of mercy and tenderness toward sinners, my own heart is filled with joy and confidence that I shall be so kindly welcomed by You. Unfortunately, how many times have I sinned! But now, with Peter and with Magdalene, I weep for my sins and detest them because they offend You, infinite Goodness. Mercifully grant me pardon for them all; and let me die rather than offend You again; at least let me live only to love You in return. Amen. (Raccolta n. 255)

Another Traditional Prayer of Reparation

My loving Jesus, out of the grateful love I bear You, and to make reparation for my unfaithfulness to grace, I give You my heart, and I consecrate myself wholly to You; and with Your help I purpose to sin no more. Amen. (Raccolta, n. 260)

Prayer To Ask the Graces Necessary for a Religious Vocation

O Lord, do not permit me to violate or neglect the observance of my holy rules. I choose Thy Sacred Heart for my dwelling, in order that It may be my strength in combat, the support of my weakness, my light and my guide in darkness, in fine, the Reparation for all my faults, the Sanctifier of all my intentions and actions, which I unite to Thine and offer Thee to serve as a continual preparation for receiving Thee. Amen.

Center of Our Hearts (by St. Claude de la Colombiere)

O God, what will you do to conquer the fearful hardness of our hearts? Lord, You must give us new hearts, tender hearts, sensitive hearts, to replace hearts that are made of marble and of bronze.

You must give us Your own Heart, Jesus. Come, lovable Heart of Jesus. Place Your Heart deep in the center of our hearts and enkindle in each heart a flame of love as strong, as great, as the sum of all the reasons that I have for loving You, my God.

O holy Heart of Jesus, dwell hidden in my heart, so that I may live only in You and only for You, so that, in the end, I may live with you eternally in Heaven. Amen.

Prayers by Fr. John A. Hardon, *SJ*

Heart of Your Mercy

Humbly prostrate at the foot of Your holy cross, I will often say to You in order to move the Heart of Your Mercy to pardon me:

Jesus, unknown and despised,
Jesus, calumniated and persecuted,
Jesus, abandoned by men and tempted,
Jesus, betrayed and sold for a vile price,
Jesus, blamed, accused, and unjustly condemned,
Jesus, clothed with a garment of opprobrium and shame,
Jesus, buffeted and mocked,
Jesus, dragged with a rope round Your neck,
Jesus, scourged unto blood,
Jesus, reputed to be a fool and to be possessed by a devil,
Jesus, to whom Barabbas was preferred,
Jesus, shamefully stripped of Your garments,
Jesus, crowned with thorns and saluted in derision,
Jesus, laden with the cross, and with the maledictions of the people,
Jesus, overwhelmed with insults, sorrow, and humiliations,
Jesus, sorrowful unto death,
Jesus, insulted, spat upon, beaten, outraged, and scoffed at,
Jesus, hanged on the infamous tree in company with robbers,
Jesus, set at naught and deprived of honor before men,
Jesus, overwhelmed with all kinds of sorrow.

O good Jesus, who has suffered an infinity of insults and humiliations for love of me, imprint the appreciation and love of them on my heart and make me desire to endure them. Amen.

Eucharistic Heart

O most sacred, most loving Heart of Jesus, Thou art concealed in the Holy Eucharist, and Thou beatest for us still. Now as then, thou sayest, "With desire, I have desired." I worship Thee, then, with all my best love and awe, with my fervent affection, with my most subdued, most resolved will.

O my God, when Thou dost condescend to suffer me to receive Thee, to eat and drink Thee, and Thou for a while takest up Thy abode within me, O make my heart beat with Thy Heart. Purify it of all that is earthly, all that is proud and sensual, all that is hard and cruel, of all perversity, of all disorder, of all deadness. So fill it with Thee, that neither the events of the day nor the circumstances of the time may have power to ruffle it, but that in Thy love and Thy fear it may have peace. Amen.

Sacred Heart Novena

Hail, O Sacred Heart of Jesus, living and animating source of eternal life, infinite treasure of the Divinity, burning furnace of divine love. Our amiable Savior, consume our hearts with that burning love with which Yours is ever inflamed. Pour down on our souls those graces which flow from Your love, and let our hearts be so united with Yours, that our wills may be one, and in all things conformed to Yours. May Yours be the standard and rule of our desires and of our actions.
V. O sweetest Heart of Jesus, we implore,
R. That we may ever love You more and more.

A Prayer of Oblation for Holy Hour or at the Offertory of Mass

My dearest Guardian Angel, please take to Our Lady of Sorrows, who stands at the foot of the Holy Cross, my heart. Ask Her for me to please purify it and create deep wells within it. Please beseech Her to present it to Our Lord and ask that it might be filled with His Most Precious Blood, which is perfect love, and the gift of Wisdom.

My dearest Guardian Angel, please, I beseech thee, take my self-will to Our Lady of Sorrows who stands at the foot of the Holy Cross. Beg Her on my behalf to crush it as She would crush the head of Satan; and present my will to Our Lord and Master as an empty vessel that He may fill with whatever He desires.

My dearest Guardian Angel, please, I beseech thee, take all of the remaining spiritual and temporal gifts, given to me by Our Lord, to Our Lady of Sorrows who stands at the foot of the Holy Cross. Ask Her on my behalf to please purify them and present them to Her Divine Son as my offering this day.

I thank Thee, My Lady Immaculate, My Lady of Perfect Charity, My Mother, and I offer these three humble Aves (Hail Mary's) in Thanksgiving for Your great kindness in hearing and answering my petition.

3 Ave Marias (3 Hail Mary's) Amen.

Part 3: Prayers of Petition

End the Holy Hour with 3 -5 minutes of petitions.

Please include a prayer for the Holy Father, your bishop, your priests, as well all favors you request.

Conclude with:

Mary, Queen of Confessors, pray for us.

St. Pius X, pray for us.

St. Alphonsus Liguori, pray for us.

St. Jean Vianney, pray for us.

Printed in the USA
CPSIA information can be obtained
at www.ICGtesting.com
LVHW060925100324
774064LV00001B/9